little **party** eats

little party eats

delectable dips, nibbles and bites for festive occasions

southwater

This edition is published by Southwater

Southwater is an imprint of Anness Publishing Ltd

Hermes House, 88–89 Blackfriars Road, London SE1 8HA

tel. 020 7401 2077; fax 020 7633 9499

© Anness Publishing Ltd 1997, 2002

Published in the USA by Southwater, Anness Publishing Inc., 27 West 20th Street, New York, NY 10011; fax 212 807 6813; www.southwaterbooks.com; info@anness.com

This edition distributed in the UK by The Manning Partnership Ltd, 6 The Old Dairy, Melcombe Road, Bath BA2 3LR; tel. 01225 478 444; fax 01225 478 440; sales@manning-partnership.co.uk

This edition distributed in the USA by National Book Network, 4720 Boston Way, Lanham, MD 20706; tel. 301 459 3366; fax 301 459 1705; www.nbnbooks.com

This edition distributed in Canada by General Publishing, 895 Don Mills Road, 400–402 Park Centre, Toronto, Ontario M3C 1W3; tel. 416 445 3333; fax 416 445 5991; www.genpub.com

This edition distributed in Australia by Pan Macmillan Australia, Level 18, St Martins Tower, 31 Market St, Sydney, NSW 2000; tel. 1300 135 113; fax 1300 135 103; email customer.service@macmillan.com.au

This edition distributed in New Zealand by The Five Mile Press (NZ) Ltd, PO Box 33–1071 Takapuna, Unit 11/101–111 Diana Drive, Glenfield, Auckland 10; tel. (09) 444 4144; fax (09) 444 4518; fivemilenz@clear.net.nz

All rights reserved. No part of this publication may be reproduced, stored in a retrieval system, or transmitted in any way or by any means, electronic, mechanical, photocopying, recording or otherwise, without the prior written permission of the copyright holder.

A CIP catalogue record for this book is available from the British Library.

Publisher   Joanna Lorenz
Managing Editor   Linda Fraser
Series Editor   Sarah Ainley
Copy Editor   Jenni Fleetwood
Designers   Patrick McLeavey & Partners
Illustrator   Anna Koska
Photographers   Karl Adamson, Edward Allwright, Steve Baxter & Amanda Heywood

Recipes   Carla Capalbo, Jacqueline Clark, Carole Clements, Joanna Farrow, Christine France & Elizabeth Wolf-Cohen

Previously published as *The Perfect Party Food Book*

For all recipes, quantities are given in both metric and imperial measures, and, where appropriate, measures are also given in standard cups and spoons. Follow one set, but not a mixture, because they are not interchangeable.

10 9 8 7 6 5 4 3 2 1

Contents

Introduction 6

Dips & Nibbles 12

Finger Foods 22

Salads & Side Dishes 34

Main Buffet Dishes 42

Party Desserts 56

Index 64

Introduction

It seemed such a good idea at the time. Let's have a party, you blithely suggested, and within a few days the whole thing has snowballed. Everyone you've asked is able to come, the event is scheduled for next Friday and you haven't a clue about what you are going to serve or how you are going to serve it.

Don't panic. The first thing to do is to kick off your shoes and settle down on the sofa with The Perfect Party Food Book. Within these pages you'll find valuable advice on planning, as well as recipes for snacks selected for easy eatability, main dishes and salads any buffet table would be proud to bear, and desserts that will delight. Much of the food can be prepared ahead, ensuring that you have plenty of time for the important things — like mingling, mixing drinks and making sure everyone has a good time.

Great parties start with careful preparation. Although it is tempting to invite everyone to whom you owe dinner, if a party is viewed principally as a payback, you may end up with a disparate group. Try to make sure at least one of the early arrivals is a good mixer, who will introduce any isolated guests to those people who all know each other, and detail someone to answer the door and take coats so that you don't have to keep disappearing.

Dips, nibbles and finger foods are great ice-breakers. It's hard to be stuffy when you're fighting over the last filo pastry or trying to lick your fingers discreetly after savouring a spare rib. Offer a selection, from simple tapas to

INTRODUCTION

onion tarts, but make sure everything can be eaten with ease and keep cocktail sticks and napkins within reach.

You could even involve the guests in the preparation of the snacks. Hot and Spicy Popcorn, for instance, positively invites audience participation. Ask one or two partygoers to pop the corn and the kitchen will soon become a magnet for others, eager to offer advice and recall popcorn-making sessions of their youth. With this type of edible entertainment, there'll be no need for party games.

When it comes to the main attraction, a buffet is the simplest solution. Choose dishes that complement each other in terms of flavour and colour, are easy to serve and eat, and are suitable for the season. A whole salmon makes an impressive centrepiece and is not outrageously expensive, now that farmed salmon is so freely available. Offer at least one vegetarian dish (keep another in reserve as vegetarian dishes are often the first to disappear) and make sure that anyone with specific dietary requirements is catered for.

This goes for desserts, too. Although most guests throw caution to the winds when it comes to party puddings, and the Chocolate Mandarin Trifle will probably come top of the popularity poll, it is only fair to offer a low-fat alternative, such as the Cool Green Fruit Salad; provide a large bowl of fresh fruit as an additional option.

Most of all, you should take the time to enjoy yourself. Parties are all about having fun – and that goes for the host most of all.

Introduction

Perfect Party Planning

INVITATIONS
Written invitations may seem a bit formal, but guests are less likely to forget if they have a piece of paper to pin up or stick on the fridge. Do ask people to RSVP, especially at peak party times like Christmas and New Year, so that you know how many to cater for.

THEMES
Suit the celebration to the season. Try a summer brunch in the garden, starting with Strawberries with Cointreau, or a late afternoon barbecue after a walk on the beach. In winter, simply offer several different types of soup, with an assortment of breads and rolls. Have an Italian night, including Parmesan Filo Triangles, Party Pizza and Baked Vegetable Lasagne, or match Mexican food with Margueritas. The possibilities for partying are endless.

NIBBLES
Juggling plates, cutlery and a glass of wine is no fun, so keep nibbles simple and easy to eat. Finger foods, like Mini Sausage Rolls, Celery Sticks with Roquefort and Tiny Cheese Puffs, are perfect. Provide bowls or mini-bins for any debris, such as cocktail sticks or olive stones.

DIPS
Simple, but always popular, dips are delicious with crudités, crisps, breadsticks or roasted potato skins. Keep one or two extras in the fridge in case refills are required. If you don't use them, serve them next day as toppings for jacket potatoes.

Introduction

MAIN DISHES

Cook as much of the main course as possible in advance, as this will often be the most time-consuming to prepare. Many guests like to mix and match the dishes on offer, so make sure at least some of them are complementary. Remember to serve at least one vegetarian option.

DRESSINGS

Like sauces, these are best served separately. Although it is tempting to make your own mayonnaise for a special occasion, if it is to stand on a buffet for any length of time, it is wiser to use a good quality bought mayonnaise.

SALADS

Don't make too much salad – at a party, people always eat less salad than you might suppose. A large iceberg lettuce, tossed with sliced cucumber, green pepper and spring onions, will easily serve 25 as part of a buffet. Use additional salads of cured meats, vegetables and rice to add colour and crunch, but keep them small.

DRINKS

Bring-a-bottle is very much the accepted practice at many parties, but you should still provide a supply of drinks for your guests. A balanced selection of drinks includes wine and beer, with soft drinks and fruit juices for drivers and those who prefer not to drink alcohol. Bottled water is always popular and tastes all the better chilled, with a slice of lemon or lime. Cocktails are great fun, but often highly alcoholic, so save them for occasions when the guests stay over. Coffee should be available, but don't feel obliged to serve it yourself on a tray; most guests will be more than willing to make their own.

INTRODUCTION

Techniques

MAKING DECORATIVE ICE CUBES
Half fill an ice cube tray with water. Freeze until solid, then top each cube with a single cranberry, olive, halved grape, raisin, shaped piece of lemon rind, mint leaf or borage flower dipped in cold water. Freeze again, then top with water and freeze again.

MAKING LEMON TWISTS
Slice a fresh lemon with a sharp knife. Cut from the peel to the centre of the lemon slice, then twist to make an "S" shape.

FROSTING GLASSES OR DISHES
Rub the rim of a glass or dish with the cut surface of a lemon or orange, then dip the rim once or twice in caster sugar or salt, to coat. Stand the glass or bowl upright and leave until the sugar or salt has dried.

STONING OLIVES
Place the base of the olive on the base of an olive stoner, with the plunger over the top. Press firmly to eject the stone. Olives are also available ready-stoned, from supermarkets.

INTRODUCTION

Great Garnishes

CARROT CURL
Roll a thin strip of carrot into a curl. Secure with a cocktail stick. Place in iced water for about 1 hour to keep the shape.

CHIVE BRAIDS
Fresh chives can be braided together up to 1–2 days ahead and kept on damp kitchen paper, in an airtight box in the fridge, until needed.

CHOCOLATE LEAVES
Choose leaves that are nicely shaped, with well-defined veins. Holly leaves work very well, as do rose leaves, but avoid poisonous leaves. Lightly brush the leaves with sunflower oil, then brush with melted dark chocolate, to make a coating 3mm/$\frac{1}{8}$in thick. Chill until set, then peel away the real leaves. Prepare up to 1 month in advance and store in a cool place, in airtight containers.

CUCUMBER BUTTERFLY
Cut a 1cm/$\frac{1}{2}$in piece of cucumber in half lengthways, then cut each semi-circular piece into 7 slices, leaving them attached at one edge. Fold every other slice back on itself to form a butterfly shape.

GHERKIN FAN
Use a sharp knife to make several cuts down the length of a gherkin. Fan out and flatten.

RADISH ROSE
Remove the stalk from the radish. Use the tip of a sharp knife to cut petal shapes around the bottom half of the radish, keeping the petals joined at the base. Cut second and third rows of petals above. Leave in iced water until the petals open.

SPRING ONION TASSEL
Trim a spring onion to 7.5cm/3in. Cut lengthways through the green part to within 4cm/1$\frac{1}{2}$in of the white end. Place the tassel in iced water until the ends begin to curl.

HOST'S HINT

Party food should look as good as it tastes. Garnishes made early in the day will keep well if spaced well apart on a tray, covered with clear film and chilled in the fridge.

Dips & Nibbles

Pepper Dips with Crudités

Ingredients

2 red peppers, halved and seeded
2 yellow peppers, halved and seeded
2 garlic cloves
30ml/2 tbsp lemon juice
20ml/4 tsp olive oil
50g/2oz/1 cup fresh white breadcrumbs
salt and ground black pepper

Crudités
celery sticks, cauliflower florets, cherry tomatoes, chicory leaves, baby button mushrooms, thin wedges of red, yellow and green peppers, courgette sticks

Serves 4–6

1 Place the red and yellow peppers in separate saucepans, adding a whole peeled garlic clove to each. Add just enough water to cover, bring to the boil, then lower the heat, cover and simmer for 15 minutes until tender.

2 Drain the red peppers, tip them into a food processor or blender and add half the lemon juice and half the olive oil. Purée, then scrape the mixture into a bowl. Treat the yellow peppers in the same way.

3 Stir half the breadcrumbs into each bowl and season to taste with salt and ground black pepper. Place the crudités on a large platter and surround them with the pepper dips, to serve.

Host's Hint
To give yourself more time on the day of the party, make the dips up to 2 days in advance, and store them in separate sealed containers, in the fridge, until needed.

Guacamole with Chilli Chips

Ingredients

2 ripe avocados
juice of 1 lime
½ small onion, finely chopped
½ fresh red chilli, seeded and finely chopped
3 tomatoes, peeled, seeded and chopped
2.5ml/½ tsp chopped fresh coriander
30ml/2 tbsp soured cream
salt and ground black pepper
15ml/1 tbsp soured cream and a pinch of cayenne pepper, to garnish

Chilli Chips
150g/5oz bag tortilla chips
25g/1oz/¼ cup finely grated mature Cheddar cheese
1.5ml/¼ tsp chilli powder
10ml/2 tsp chopped fresh parsley

Serves 4

1 Cut the avocados in half and remove the stone from each. Scrape the flesh from the shells into a food processor or blender.

2 Add the lime juice, onion, chilli, tomatoes, fresh coriander and the soured cream to the avocados, with salt and ground black pepper to taste. Pulse the mixture until fairly smooth. Transfer to a bowl, then cover the surface of the guacamole closely with clear film and chill in the fridge.

3 Make the chips. Preheat the grill. Scatter the tortilla chips over a baking sheet. In a bowl, mix the grated cheese with the chilli powder. Sprinkle the mixture over the chips and grill for 1–2 minutes until the cheese has melted.

4 Remove the guacamole from the fridge and swirl the soured cream over the top. Sprinkle with the cayenne pepper. Place the guacamole on a serving plate and surround it with the chilli chips sprinkled with chopped fresh parsley.

Hot Crab Dip

Ingredients

225g/8oz/1 cup cream cheese, at room temperature
30–45ml/2–3 tbsp milk
15ml/1 tbsp brandy or vermouth
2 spring onions, finely chopped
5–10ml/1–2 tsp Dijon mustard
salt
2–3 dashes of Tabasco sauce
15ml/1 tbsp finely chopped fresh dill or parsley
225g/8oz white crab meat, picked over
45–60ml/3–4 tbsp flaked almonds

Serves 6

1 Preheat the oven to 190°C/375°F/Gas 5. In a large mixing bowl, beat the cream cheese with the milk, brandy or vermouth, chopped spring onions and mustard. Add salt and Tabasco sauce to taste, then stir in the chopped fresh herbs and crab meat.

2 Spoon the mixture into a small gratin or baking dish and sprinkle the almonds over the top. Bake in the preheated oven for 12–15 minutes, until the top is golden and the crab mixture is hot and bubbling. Serve the dip at once, with savoury biscuits or fingers of hot toast.

Host's Hint

For a pretty party platter, bake the crab dip in tomato shells. Choose small (but not cherry) tomatoes, squeeze out the seeds and carefully remove the pulp. Drain the shells upside down on kitchen paper, then fill them with the crab mixture, minus the almonds.
Bake for 8–10 minutes.

Celery Sticks with Roquefort

INGREDIENTS

200g/7oz/generous 1 cup Roquefort or other blue cheese, softened
275g/10oz/1¼ cups low-fat soft cheese
2 spring onions, finely chopped
ground black pepper
15–30ml/1–2 tbsp milk (optional)
1 celery head, separated into stalks
chopped walnuts or hazelnuts, to garnish

SERVES 10–12

3 If necessary, peel the celery stalks lightly to remove any heavy strings. Cut each stalk into 7.5–10cm/3–4in pieces. Using a small knife, fill each celery stick  with a little of the cheese mixture. Press on a few chopped nuts. Arrange on a serving plate and chill in the fridge until ready to serve.

1 Crumble the Roquefort or other blue cheese into a small bowl. Mash it lightly with a fork, then tip it into a food processor. Add the soft cheese, chopped spring onions and a generous grinding of pepper.

2 Process the mixture until smooth, occasionally scraping down the sides of the bowl, and adding milk if the mixture seems too stiff.

Tapas of Almonds, Olives and Cheese

Ingredients

Marinated Olives
2.5ml / ½ tsp coriander seeds
2.5ml / ½ tsp fennel seeds
5ml / 1 tsp chopped fresh rosemary
10ml / 2 tsp chopped fresh parsley
2 garlic cloves, crushed
15ml / 1 tbsp sherry vinegar
30ml / 2 tbsp olive oil
115g / 4oz / ⅔ cup black olives
115g / 4oz / ⅔ cup green olives
Marinated Cheese
150g / 5oz goat's cheese, preferably manchego
3 fresh tarragon or thyme sprigs
90ml / 6 tbsp olive oil
15ml / 1 tbsp white wine vinegar
5ml / 1 tsp black peppercorns
1 garlic clove, sliced
fresh tarragon sprigs, to garnish
Salted Almonds
1.5ml / ¼ tsp cayenne pepper
30ml / 2 tbsp sea salt
25g / 1oz / 2 tbsp butter
60ml / 4 tbsp olive oil
200g / 7oz / 1¾ cups blanched almonds
extra sea salt for sprinkling (optional)

Serves 6–8

1 Marinate the olives. Mix the coriander and fennel seeds in a mortar and crush finely with a pestle. Add the rosemary, parsley, garlic, vinegar and oil. Mix well. Put the olives in a bowl, pour the marinade over, cover and chill for up to 1 week.

2 Marinate the cheese. Cut the cheese into bite-size pieces, leaving the rind on. Place in a small bowl with the herb sprigs. Mix the oil, vinegar, peppercorns and garlic. Pour over the cheese, cover and chill for up to 3 days.

3 Make the salted almonds. Mix the cayenne and salt in a shallow bowl. Melt the butter with the olive oil in a frying pan. Add the almonds and fry, stirring, for 5 minutes or until golden.

4 Tip the almonds into the spiced salt and toss to coat. Leave to cool, then store in an airtight jar for up to 1 week. To serve the tapas, arrange them in separate dishes. Garnish the cheese with fresh tarragon sprigs and scatter the almonds with a little more salt, if you like.

Tiny Cheese Puffs

INGREDIENTS

115g/4oz/1 cup plain flour
2.5ml/½ tsp salt
5ml/1 tsp dry mustard
pinch of cayenne pepper
250ml/8fl oz/1 cup water
115g/4oz/½ cup butter, diced
4 eggs
75g/3oz Gruyère cheese, finely diced
15ml/1 tbsp snipped fresh chives

MAKES ABOUT 45

1 Preheat the oven to 200°C/400°F/Gas 6. Lightly grease two large baking sheets. Sift the flour, salt, mustard and cayenne pepper into a bowl.

2 In a medium saucepan, heat the water and butter until the butter melts, then bring to the boil. Remove from the heat and add the flour all at once, beating with a wooden spoon until the dough forms a ball that leaves the sides of the pan. Return to the heat and beat constantly for 1–2 minutes to dry out. Cool for 3–5 minutes.

3 Beat three of the eggs into the dough, adding them one at a time and beating well after each addition. Beat the fourth egg in a cup and add a teaspoon at a time, beating until the dough is shiny and drops slowly from the spoon. (You may not need all of the fourth egg; save the rest for glazing.) Stir in the diced cheese and chives.

4 Using two teaspoons, drop small mounds of the dough, 5cm/2in apart, on the baking sheets. Beat the remaining egg with about 15ml/1 tbsp water and glaze the tops of the mounds. Bake for about 8 minutes, then lower the oven temperature to 180°C/350°F/Gas 4 and bake for 7–8 minutes more until puffed and golden. Allow to cool slightly on a wire rack, then serve.

Hot & Spicy Popcorn

INGREDIENTS

120ml/4fl oz/½ cup vegetable oil, plus extra for popping
175g/6oz/1 cup popping corn
2–3 garlic cloves, bruised
5–10ml/1–2 tsp chilli powder (or to taste)
pinch of cayenne pepper
salt

MAKES ABOUT 175G/6OZ/12 CUPS

1 Heat the oil for popping in a deep, heavy-based saucepan. Pop the corn according to the instructions on the packet. Cover the pan with a lid until the corn has finished popping.

2 In a small saucepan, combine the measured oil, garlic, chilli powder and cayenne. Stir over a gentle heat for about 5 minutes, to blend the flavours, then lift out the garlic cloves with a slotted spoon.

3 Pour the flavoured oil over the popcorn and toss well. Season with salt to taste. Tip the popcorn into a large bowl and serve warm or at room temperature.

VARIATION
For Parmesan Popcorn, omit the chilli powder and salt from the flavoured oil. Pour the hot oil over the popcorn, toss to coat, then add 90ml/6 tbsp grated Parmesan cheese and toss again until coated.

Finger Foods

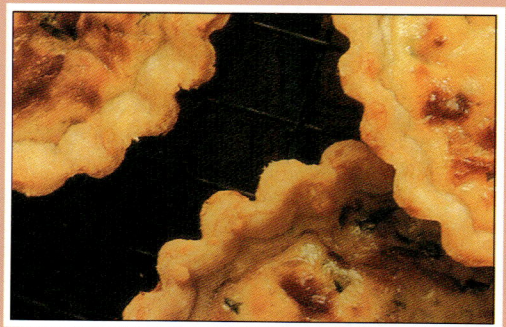

Mini Sausage Rolls

INGREDIENTS

15g/½oz/1 tbsp butter
1 onion, finely chopped
350g/12oz good quality sausagemeat
15ml/1 tbsp dried mixed herbs
25g/1oz/⅓ cup finely chopped pistachio nuts (optional)
350g/12oz puff pastry, thawed if frozen
60–90ml/4–6 tbsp grated Parmesan cheese
salt and ground black pepper
beaten egg, for glazing
poppy seeds, sesame seeds, fennel seeds or aniseeds, for sprinkling
fresh dill, to garnish

MAKES ABOUT 48

1 Melt the butter in a small frying pan and fry the onion over a medium heat for about 5 minutes, until softened. Tip into a bowl and cool, then add the sausagemeat and herbs, with plenty of salt and pepper. Add the nuts, if using, and mix well.

2 Divide the sausage mixture into four equal portions and roll each to a thin 25cm/10in sausage. On a lightly floured surface, roll out the pastry thinly and cut it into four strips, each measuring 25 x 7.5cm/10 x 3in. Place a "sausage" on each strip and sprinkle with Parmesan.

3 Brush one long edge of each pastry strip with egg and roll up to enclose the filling. Set the rolls seam-side down and press gently to seal. Brush with more egg and sprinkle with seeds.

4 Preheat the oven to 220°C/425°F/Gas 7. Lightly grease a large baking sheet. Cut each pastry log into 2.5cm/1in lengths and arrange on the baking sheet. Bake for 15 minutes, until the pastry is crisp and brown. Serve warm, with a dill garnish.

Roasted Garlic Toasts

INGREDIENTS

2 whole heads of garlic
extra virgin olive oil (see method)
fresh rosemary sprigs
ciabatta loaf or thick baguette
chopped fresh rosemary
salt and ground black pepper

MAKES 10–12

3 Squeeze the garlic cloves out of their skins on to the toasts, spread with a knife to coat the toasts, then sprinkle with the chopped fresh rosemary. Drizzle  a little more olive oil over, if you like. Add salt and ground black pepper to taste and serve hot.

1 Keep the heads of the garlic intact and unpeeled and slice off the tops with a sharp knife. Brush each head generously with olive oil, then wrap in foil with  a few rosemary sprigs and place on a baking sheet. Grill under a medium heat for 25–30 minutes, turning occasionally, until soft.

2 Slice the bread at a slight angle and brush each slice generously with olive oil. Toast under the grill until golden, turning once.

Parmesan Filo Triangles

INGREDIENTS

olive oil, for brushing
3 large sheets of filo pastry
45–60ml/3–4 tbsp grated Parmesan cheese
2.5ml/½ tsp crumbled dried thyme or sage

MAKES ABOUT 24

1 Preheat the oven to 180°C/350°F/Gas 4. Line a large baking sheet with foil and brush it lightly with oil. Keeping the rest of the filo covered, lay one sheet on a work surface and brush lightly with oil. Sprinkle with half the Parmesan and a little dried thyme or sage.

2 Cover with a second filo sheet, brush with oil and add the remaining Parmesan and dried herbs. Top with the remaining sheet of filo, then brush it very lightly with oil.

3 Using a sharp knife, cut the stack of filo sheets in half lengthways. Carefully cut them into squares, then cut each square in half to make two triangles.

4 Arrange the triangles, widely spaced, on the baking sheet, scrunching them slightly. Bake in the preheated oven for 6–8 minutes until the filos are crisp and golden. Allow to cool slightly and serve.

Onion & Goat's Cheese Tartlets

Ingredients

350g/12oz/3 cups plain flour
150g/5oz/⅔ cup butter
50g/2oz hard goat's cheese or
Cheddar cheese, grated

Filling
30–45ml/2–3 tbsp olive oil
4 onions, finely chopped
350g/12oz/1½ cups soft goat's cheese
3 eggs, beaten
30ml/2 tbsp single cream
115g/4oz hard goat's cheese, grated
30ml/2 tbsp chopped fresh tarragon
salt and ground black pepper

Makes 16–20

1 Sift the flour into a mixing bowl. Rub in the butter until the mixture resembles breadcrumbs, then stir in the grated cheese. Add enough cold water to make a dough. Knead lightly, wrap in clear film and chill in the fridge. Preheat the oven to 190°C/375°F/Gas 5.

2 Roll out the pastry on a lightly floured surface and cut into 16–20 rounds to fit patty tins. Prick the bases with a fork. Bake for about 10–15 minutes until firm but not browned. Remove the pastry cases and lower the oven temperature to 180°C/350°F/Gas 4.

3 Make the filling. Heat the oil in a large frying pan. Fry the chopped onions over a low heat for 20–25 minutes until they are golden brown. Stir occasionally to prevent them from burning.

4 Beat the soft goat's cheese in a bowl, then add the eggs, cream, hard goat's cheese and tarragon. Season with salt and pepper, then stir in the fried onions.

5 Divide the mixture between the pastry cases. Bake for 20–25 minutes, until golden. Serve warm.

Blinis with Smoked Salmon & Dill Cream

INGREDIENTS

225g/8oz/2 cups buckwheat flour
225g/8oz/2 cups plain flour
2.5ml/½ tsp salt
20ml/4 tsp easy-blend dried yeast
4 eggs
750ml/1¼ pints/3 cups hand-hot milk
25g/1oz/2 tbsp butter, melted, plus extra for frying
300ml/½ pint/1¼ cups crème fraîche
75ml/5 tbsp chopped fresh dill
450g/1lb thinly sliced smoked salmon
fresh dill sprigs, to garnish

SERVES 12

1 Mix the buckwheat and plain flours in a large mixing bowl. Add the salt and yeast and mix well. Separate 2 of the eggs. Whisk the whole eggs with the egg yolks, hand-hot milk and melted butter in a large jug.

2 Pour the egg mixture on to the flour mixture and beat to a smooth batter. Cover and leave to rise in a warm place for 1–2 hours.

3 Whisk the egg whites in a clean grease-free bowl until stiff, then gently fold into the batter. Preheat a heavy-based frying pan and brush with the extra melted butter. Drop tablespoons of the batter into the frying pan, spacing them well apart. Cook the spoonfuls of batter until bubbles appear on the surface.

4 Flip the blinis over and cook for about 30 seconds on the other side. Keep warm while cooking successive batches, buttering the pan each time. Mix together the crème fraîche and dill in a large bowl. Top the blinis with the sliced smoked salmon. Add a swirl of dill cream and a sprig of fresh dill to each blini, to serve.

Spicy Chicken Wings

INGREDIENTS

16 plump chicken wings
4 large garlic cloves, cut into slivers
30ml/2 tbsp olive oil
30ml/2 tbsp paprika
10ml/2 tsp chilli powder
10ml/2 tsp dried oregano
5ml/1 tsp salt
5ml/1 tsp ground black pepper
fresh lime wedges, to serve

MAKES 16

1 Using a small, sharp knife, make one or two cuts in the skin of each chicken wing and carefully slide a sliver of garlic under the skin. Brush the wings with the olive oil.

2 Mix the paprika, chilli powder, oregano, salt and pepper in a large bowl or stout polythene bag. Add the chicken wings and toss until they are lightly coated.

3 Spread out the chicken wings in a grill pan and grill under a moderately high heat for about 15 minutes, until they are cooked through, and the skin is crisp and blackened. Serve the chicken wings with fresh lime wedges.

HOST'S HINT

Bake the chicken wings, if you prefer. They will need 30–35 minutes in an oven preheated to 190°C/375°F/Gas 5.

Skewered Lamb with Red Onion Salsa

INGREDIENTS

225g/8oz lean lamb, cubed
2.5ml/½ tsp ground cumin
2.5ml/½ tsp ground paprika
15ml/1 tbsp olive oil
salt and ground black pepper

SALSA

1 red onion, very thinly sliced
1 large ripe tomato, seeded and chopped
15ml/1 tbsp red wine vinegar
3–4 fresh basil or mint leaves, roughly torn
small fresh mint leaves, to garnish

SERVES 4

2 Drain the skewers and thread them with the lamb, spacing the cubes slightly apart so that they cook evenly.

3 Make the salsa by mixing the onion, tomato and vinegar in a small bowl. Add the fresh herb leaves and stir well. Season with salt to taste, garnish with  the whole mint leaves and set aside to allow the flavours to blend.

4 Cook the lamb under a moderately hot grill for 5–10 minutes, turning the skewers often, until the lamb is well browned on the outside, but still slightly pink in the centre. Serve hot, with the salsa.

1 Soak four small wooden skewers in cold water for at least 30 minutes to prevent scorching. Place the lamb cubes in a bowl and add the cumin, paprika  and olive oil. Grind over plenty of salt and black pepper. Toss well until the lamb is coated with the spice mix.

HOST'S HINT

For a crowd, simply multiply the ingredients according to the number of guests expected. The kebabs are delicious if cooked over a barbecue, so this is an excellent choice for a summer barbecue party.

Tandoori Chicken Sticks

INGREDIENTS

450g/1lb chicken breasts, skinned and boned
coriander yogurt, to serve

MARINADE
175ml/6fl oz/¾ cup natural yogurt
5ml/1 tsp garam masala
1.5ml/¼ tsp ground cumin
1.5ml/¼ tsp ground coriander
1.5ml/¼ tsp cayenne pepper (or to taste)
5ml/1 tsp tomato purée
1–2 garlic cloves, finely chopped
2.5cm/½in piece of fresh root ginger, peeled and finely chopped
grated rind and juice of ½ lemon
15–30ml/1–2 tbsp chopped fresh coriander or mint

MAKES ABOUT 25

1 Make the marinade by processing all of the ingredients together in a food processor until smooth. Pour into a large, shallow dish.

2 Freeze the chicken breasts for 5 minutes to firm the flesh, then slice in half horizontally. Cut the slices into 2cm/¾in strips and add to the marinade. Toss to coat well. Cover and chill for 6–8 hours or overnight.

3 Line a large baking sheet with foil. Using a slotted spoon, remove the chicken from the marinade and arrange the pieces in a single layer on the foil-lined sheet. Scrunch up the chicken slightly, so that it makes wavy shapes.

4 Grill the marinated chicken for 4–5 minutes until brown and just cooked, turning once. Thread 1–2 pieces on cocktail sticks and serve hot, with the coriander yogurt as a dipping sauce.

Barbecued Mini Ribs

Ingredients

1 sheet of pork ribs, about 675g/1½lb
30ml/2 tbsp plain flour, seasoned with salt and ground black pepper
90ml/6 tbsp sweet sherry
15ml/1 tbsp tomato purée
5ml/1 tsp soy sauce
2.5ml/½ tsp Tabasco sauce
15ml/1 tbsp light muscovado sugar
coarse sea salt

MAKES ABOUT 30 PIECES

1 Separate the ribs, then, using a heavy knife, cut each rib in half widthways, to make about 30 pieces. Put the seasoned flour in a stout plastic bag, add the ribs and toss to coat.

2 Mix the sherry, tomato purée, soy sauce, Tabasco and sugar in a small bowl. Stir in 2.5ml/½ tsp salt.

3 Dip each floured rib separately in the sherry sauce, arrange on a grill rack and place under a hot grill for 30–40 minutes, until cooked through and a little charred on the outside. Sprinkle with sea salt and serve at once.

Host's Hint

These are literally finger-lickin' tasty, but it is a good idea to provide finger bowls and a stack of paper napkins for more fastidious guests.

Salads & Side Dishes

Avocado, Orange & Almond Salad

Ingredients

2 oranges
2 well-flavoured tomatoes
30ml/2 tbsp lemon juice
15ml/1 tbsp chopped fresh parsley
60ml/4 tbsp extra virgin olive oil
2 small avocados
1 small onion, sliced into rings
salt and ground black pepper

Garnish

25g/1oz/¼ cup flaked almonds
10–12 black olives

Serves 8

1 Peel the oranges, taking care to remove all the pith. Slice them into thick rounds. Peel the tomatoes, slice them into quarters and squeeze out the seeds. Chop the tomato flesh roughly.

2 Mix the lemon juice and parsley in a bowl. Season with salt and black pepper. Whisk in the oil. Pour half the dressing into a jug and set aside.

3 Cut each avocado in half, remove the stones and peel away the skin. Cut the flesh into chunks and add to the dressing in the bowl. Add the tomatoes and toss lightly to coat.

4 Arrange the orange slices and onion rings on a plate. Drizzle with the dressing and add the avocado mixture. Garnish with almonds and olives.

Mediterranean Salad with Basil

INGREDIENTS

225g/8oz/2 cups chunky dried pasta shapes
175g/6oz fine green beans, trimmed
2 large ripe tomatoes, sliced
50g/2oz/generous 1 cup fresh basil leaves
200g/7oz can tuna in oil, drained and flaked
2 hard-boiled eggs, shelled and sliced
50g/2oz can anchovies, drained
capers and black olives, to garnish

DRESSING

30ml/2 tbsp white wine vinegar
2 garlic cloves, crushed
2.5ml/½ tsp Dijon mustard
90ml/6 tbsp extra virgin olive oil
30ml/2 tbsp snipped fresh basil
salt and ground black pepper

SERVES 8

1 Make the dressing. Mix the vinegar, garlic and mustard in a small bowl. Add the oil and whisk well, then stir in the fresh basil, with salt and ground black pepper to taste.

2 Bring a large saucepan of lightly salted water to the boil. Add the pasta and cook for 10–12 minutes, or until just tender. Drain well, tip into a bowl and cool. Blanch the beans in a small saucepan of boiling water for 3 minutes. Drain, refresh under cold water and drain again.

3 Arrange the tomato slices in the bottom of a salad bowl. Drizzle over a little of the dressing and cover with a quarter of the fresh basil leaves. Arrange the beans on top of the basil, drizzling them with more dressing, then add a third of the remaining basil leaves.

4 Add the tuna to the pasta, with half the remaining basil. Pour over a little of the dressing and toss to mix. Spoon the mixture over the salad. Arrange the  eggs and anchovies on top and garnish with the capers and olives. Pour over the remaining dressing and sprinkle with the remaining basil. Serve the salad at room temperature.

HOST'S HINT

You can make this salad a little in advance of when you will need it but don't be tempted to chill it. The fabulous freshness and flavour of the ingredients will be dulled if the salad has to sit in the fridge.

Carrot, Apple & Orange Coleslaw

INGREDIENTS

350g/12oz young carrots, grated
2 eating apples
15ml/1 tbsp lemon juice
1 large orange

DRESSING
45ml/3 tbsp olive oil
60ml/4 tbsp sunflower oil
45ml/3 tbsp lemon juice
1 garlic clove, crushed
60ml/4 tbsp natural yogurt
15ml/1 tbsp chopped mixed fresh herbs
(tarragon, parsley, chives)
salt and ground black pepper

SERVES 8

1 Place the grated carrots in a large salad bowl. Quarter both the apples, remove the core from each piece and slice the pieces thinly into a separate bowl. Sprinkle with lemon juice, to prevent discoloration, then add them to the carrots.

2 Using a sharp knife, remove the peel and pith from the orange. Working over the salad bowl to catch any juices, carefully slice between the membranes to remove the segments. Add the segments to the bowl.

3 Make the dressing. Mix all the ingredients in a screw-top jar, close the lid tightly and shake vigorously. Just before serving, pour the dressing over the salad and toss well.

Roasted Pepper Salad

Ingredients

1 red pepper
1 yellow pepper
4 sun-dried tomatoes in oil, drained
4 ripe plum tomatoes, sliced
2 canned anchovies, drained
15ml/1 tsp capers, drained
15ml/1 tbsp pine nuts
1 garlic clove, sliced into thin slivers
fresh basil leaves, to garnish

Dressing
75ml/5 tbsp extra virgin olive oil
15ml/1 tbsp balsamic vinegar
5ml/1 tsp lemon juice
chopped fresh mixed herbs
salt and ground black pepper

Serves 8

2 Slice the sun-dried tomatoes thinly. Arrange the peppers and fresh tomatoes on a serving dish, then scatter over the anchovies, sun-dried tomatoes, capers, pine nuts and garlic slices.

3 Make the dressing. Combine all the ingredients in a screw-top jar. Close the lid tightly and shake the jar vigorously to blend the ingredients. Pour the dressing over the salad 1–2 hours before serving.

1 Cut the peppers in half. Remove the seeds and stalks, then cut the peppers in quarters. Cook skin-side up under a hot grill until the skin blisters and chars.  Place in a bowl, cover with kitchen paper and leave to cool. Peel the peppers and cut them into thin strips.

Chorizos in Red Wine

INGREDIENTS

450g/1lb cured chorizo sausages
175ml/6fl oz/¾ cup red wine
60ml/4 tbsp brandy
chopped fresh parsley, to garnish

SERVES 12

1 Prick the chorizo sausages in several places with a fork. Place them in a saucepan with the wine. Bring to the boil, lower the heat, cover and simmer for 15 minutes. Remove from the heat and leave to cool, still covered, for about 2 hours.

2 Using a slotted spoon, lift the sausages out of the saucepan. On a chopping board, cut them into 1cm/½ in slices, using a sharp kitchen knife.

3 Heat a heavy-based frying pan, add the chorizo slices and toss until warmed. Pour over the brandy and carefully set it alight with a long match.

4 When the flames have died down, pour the reserved wine into the pan and cook for 2–3 minutes, until piping hot. Serve in a heated bowl, garnished with chopped parsley, and invite guests to spear the tasty chorizo slices with cocktail sticks.

Baked Tomatoes with Garlic

INGREDIENTS

8 tomatoes
90ml/6 tbsp dry breadcrumbs
3 garlic cloves, very finely chopped
60ml/4 tbsp chopped fresh parsley
60–90ml/4–6 tbsp olive oil
salt and ground black pepper
flat leaf parsley sprigs, to garnish

MAKES 16

1 Preheat the oven to 220°C/425°F/Gas 7. Line a baking sheet with foil. Cut the tomatoes in half crossways and arrange them cut-side up on the baking sheet.

2 Mix the breadcrumbs, chopped garlic and fresh parsley in a small bowl. Spoon the mixture over the tomato halves.

3 Drizzle generously with olive oil and season. Bake at the top of the oven for 8–10 minutes, until lightly browned. Serve at once, garnished with parsley sprigs.

HOST'S HINT
Use cherry tomatoes if you want to make bite-sized snacks, but make sure not to overcook them, or they will collapse.

Main Buffet Dishes

Stilton Burgers

Ingredients

900g/2lb minced beef
2 onions, finely chopped
2 celery sticks, finely chopped
10ml/2 tsp mixed herbs
10ml/2 tsp prepared mustard
115g/4oz/1 cup crumbled Stilton cheese
8 burger buns, split
salt and ground black pepper
salad and mustard pickle, to serve

Serves 8

1 Mix the beef, onions and celery in a bowl. Add plenty of salt and pepper, then stir in the herbs and mustard. Mix with a fork, then with clean hands to form a firm mixture.

2 Divide the mixture into 16 equal portions. Roll each portion into a ball, then flatten eight of the balls to form patties. Place a little of the crumbled Stilton in the centre of each patty.

3 Flatten the remaining balls of mixture and place one on top of each patty. Mould the patties together around the filling and shape them into eight plump burgers.

4 Place the burgers on a grill rack and grill under a medium heat for 10 minutes, turning once, or until cooked through. Slip inside the burger buns with salad and mustard pickle, to serve.

Tex-Mex Baked Potatoes with Chilli

Ingredients

4 large potatoes
30ml/2 tbsp oil
1 large onion, chopped
1 red pepper, seeded and chopped
2 garlic cloves, crushed
450g/1lb minced beef
1 small fresh red chilli, seeded and chopped
10ml/2 tsp ground cumin
generous pinch of cayenne pepper
400g/14oz can chopped tomatoes
60ml/4 tbsp tomato purée
120ml/4fl oz/½ cup water
5ml/1 tsp dried oregano
5ml/1 tsp dried marjoram
400g/14oz can red kidney beans, drained
30ml/2 tbsp chopped fresh coriander
salt and ground black pepper
150ml/¼ pint/⅔ cup soured cream and chopped fresh parsley, to garnish

Serves 8

1 Preheat the oven to 220°C/425°F/Gas 7. Pierce each potato with a skewer. Bake directly on the top shelf of the oven for 30 minutes before starting to cook the chilli.

2 Heat the oil in a saucepan and fry the onion, chopped red pepper and garlic for 4–5 minutes, until softened.

3 Add the beef. Fry until browned all over, then stir in the chilli, cumin, cayenne, tomatoes, tomato purée, water and herbs. Bring to the boil, then lower the heat, cover tightly and simmer for 25 minutes, stirring occasionally.

4 Add the kidney beans and heat through, stirring, for 5 minutes. Turn off the heat and add the chopped fresh coriander, with salt and ground black pepper to taste.

5 Cut the baked potatoes in half and pile them on a serving platter. Serve the chilli in a casserole and the soured cream and chopped parsley in separate bowls. Invite guests to help themselves.

Party Pizza

Ingredients

175g/6oz/1½ cups strong white flour
1.5ml/¼ tsp salt
5ml/1 tsp easy-blend dried yeast
15ml/1 tbsp olive oil
about 150ml/¼ pint/⅔ cup hand-hot water
oregano leaves, to garnish

Topping

15ml/1 tbsp olive oil
115g/4oz can peeled and chopped green chillies in brine, drained (optional)
300ml/½ pint/1¼ cups home-made tomato sauce (or a commercial equivalent)
75g/3oz sliced pepperoni
6 stoned black olives, halved lengthways
15ml/1 tbsp chopped fresh oregano
115g/4oz mozzarella cheese, grated

Serves 8

1 Sift the flour and salt into a large mixing bowl. Stir in the yeast. Make a well in the centre and add the olive oil, with enough of the hand-hot water to make a soft, malleable dough. Knead on a lightly floured surface for about 10 minutes, until smooth and elastic, then return the dough to the clean bowl, cover with clear film and leave in a warm place for about an hour, until it has doubled in bulk.

2 Preheat the oven to 220°C/425°F/Gas 7. Turn the dough on to a lightly floured surface and knead again for 2–3 minutes. Roll out to a 30cm/12in round and place on a large baking sheet. Push up the dough edges to make a rim.

3 Brush the base with the olive oil. If using the chillies, stir them into the tomato sauce. Spread over the base and scatter the pepperoni, olives and oregano on top.

4 Sprinkle the grated mozzarella over the top of the pizza. Bake in the preheated oven for 15–20 minutes, until the crust is crisp and golden. Cut the pizza into slices and serve at once, garnished with fresh oregano.

Host's Hint

Make several of these pizzas for a party, but omit the chillies from at least half of them, as they may be too hot for some guests

Tortilla Flutes

Ingredients

24 unbaked flour tortillas
2 tomatoes, peeled, seeded and chopped
1 small onion, chopped
1 garlic clove, crushed
15ml/1 tbsp corn oil, plus extra for shallow frying
salt
2 freshly cooked boneless chicken breasts, skinned and shredded
sliced radishes and stuffed green olives to garnish

Makes 12

1 Place the flour tortillas in pairs on a clean work surface, with one tortilla overlapping the other by about 5cm/2in. Purée the tomatoes with the onion and garlic in a food processor until smooth. Season the tomatoes with salt to taste.

2 Heat the measured corn oil in a frying pan and cook the tomato purée for 2–3 minutes, stirring. Off the heat, stir in the shredded chicken.

3 Spread about 30ml/2 tbsp of the chicken mixture on each pair of tortillas, then roll the tortillas into flutes and secure them with a cocktail stick.

4 Heat the oil for shallow frying in a large frying pan. Fry the flutes, in batches, until browned all over. Drain on kitchen paper and keep hot. When all the flutes have been fried, transfer them to a platter, garnish with radishes and olives, and serve.

Spinach in Filo with Three Cheeses

Ingredients

450g/1lb spinach
15ml/1 tbsp sunflower oil
15g/½oz/1 tbsp butter
1 small onion, chopped
175g/6oz ricotta cheese
115g/4oz feta cheese, cubed
75g/3oz Gruyère or Emmental cheese, grated
15ml/1 tbsp chopped fresh chervil
5ml/1 tsp chopped fresh marjoram
salt and ground black pepper
5 large or 10 small sheets filo pastry
40–50g/1½–2oz butter, melted

Serves 4

1 Preheat the oven to 190°C/375°F/Gas 5. Cook the spinach in a large saucepan over a moderate heat for 3–4 minutes until the leaves have wilted, shaking the pan occasionally. Strain and press out the excess liquid.

2 Heat the oil and butter in a frying pan and fry the onion for 3–4 minutes until softened. Remove from the heat and add half of the spinach. Combine the two ingredients, using a metal spoon to break up the spinach.

3 Add the ricotta cheese and stir until combined. Stir in the remaining spinach, again chopping it into the mixture with a metal spoon. Fold in the feta and Gruyère or Emmental, chervil, marjoram and seasoning.

4 Lay a filo sheet measuring 30cm/12in square on a clean surface. Brush with melted butter and cover with a second sheet; brush this with butter and build up five layers in this way.

5 Spread the filling over the pastry, leaving a 2.5cm/1in border around the edge. Fold the sides of the pastry inwards and then roll up.

6 Place the roll, seam side down, on a greased baking sheet and brush with the remaining butter. Bake in the preheated oven for about 30 minutes, until the filo is golden brown.

Main Buffet Dishes

Lamb Moussaka

Ingredients

900g/2lb aubergines
120ml/4fl oz/½ cup olive oil
2 large onions, sliced
450g/1lb minced lamb
2 large tomatoes, peeled and chopped
1.5ml/¼ tsp ground cinnamon
1.5ml/¼ tsp ground allspice
30ml/2 tbsp tomato purée
45ml/3 tbsp chopped fresh parsley
120ml/4fl oz/½ cup dry white wine
salt and ground black pepper
45ml/3 tbsp toasted breadcrumbs, for the topping
Sauce
50g/2oz/¼ cup butter
50g/2oz/½ cup plain flour
600ml/1 pint/2½ cups milk
1.5ml/¼ tsp grated nutmeg
25g/1oz/⅓ cup grated Parmesan cheese

Serves 8

1 Slice the aubergines and layer them in a colander, sprinkling each layer with plenty of salt. Leave to stand for 30 minutes, then rinse very thoroughly, squeeze lightly to remove the excess liquid and pat dry on kitchen paper.

2 Heat a little of the olive oil in a large frying pan. Fry the aubergine slices in batches until golden on both sides, adding more oil as needed. Drain on kitchen paper.

3 Preheat the oven to 180°C/350°F/Gas 4. Heat 30ml/2 tbsp olive oil in a saucepan. Add the onions and lamb and fry gently for 5 minutes, stirring to break up the lamb.

4 Add the tomatoes, cinnamon, allspice, tomato purée, parsley and wine, with a generous grinding of black pepper. Bring to the boil, lower the heat, cover and simmer for 15 minutes.

5 Meanwhile, make the sauce. Melt the butter in a small pan and stir in the flour. Cook for 1 minute, then gradually add the milk, stirring over a low heat until the mixture boils and thickens. Add the nutmeg and Parmesan, with salt and ground black pepper to taste.

6 Spoon alternate layers of the aubergines and meat mixture into a shallow ovenproof dish, finishing with a layer of aubergines. Pour the sauce evenly over the top and sprinkle with the breadcrumbs. Bake for about 45 minutes until the topping is golden. Serve the moussaka hot, sprinkled with extra ground black pepper, if liked.

Cheese & Onion Flan

INGREDIENTS

225g/8oz/2 cups plain flour
2.5ml/½ tsp salt
50g/2oz/¼ cup butter, diced
10ml/2 tsp easy-blend dried yeast
1 egg yolk
120ml/4fl oz/½ cup hand-hot milk
lettuce leaves and parsley, to garnish

FILLING

15g/½oz/1 tbsp butter
1 onion, halved and sliced
2 eggs
250ml/8fl oz/1 cup single cream
225g/8oz Port Salut cheese, rinded and sliced

SERVES 6–8

1 Place the flour and salt in a mixing bowl. Rub in the butter, then stir in the yeast. Add the egg yolk and hand-hot milk and mix to a dough.

2 Knead the dough on a lightly floured surface for 10 minutes, then return it to the clean bowl, cover and leave in a warm place for 1 hour or until doubled in bulk.

3 Knead the dough again briefly, then roll it out to a 30cm/12in round. Use it to line a 23cm/9in flan tin. Leave to rise again while you make the filling.

4 Melt the butter in a frying pan and fry the onion over a low heat for 15 minutes, then raise the heat and cook, stirring often, until it starts to caramelize.

5 Preheat the oven to 180°C/350°F/Gas 4. Beat the eggs and cream in a bowl, season to taste, then add the onion. Arrange the cheese on the base of the dough. Pour over the filling and bake for 30–35 minutes, until the crust is golden and the filling just set. Garnish and serve warm.

Baked Vegetable Lasagne

Ingredients

30ml/2 tbsp olive oil
1 onion, very finely chopped
2 x 400g/14oz cans chopped tomatoes with basil, drained
75g/3oz/6 tbsp butter
675g/1½lb mushrooms, thinly sliced
2 garlic cloves, crushed
juice of ½ lemon
60ml/4 tbsp chopped fresh parsley
1 litre/1¾ pints/4 cups béchamel sauce
12 sheets no-precook lasagne
175g/6oz/2 cups grated Parmesan cheese
salt and ground black pepper

Serves 8

1 Preheat the oven to 200°C/400°F/Gas 6. Heat the oil in a saucepan and fry the onion until softened. Add the chopped tomatoes and cook for 6–8 minutes, stirring frequently. Season with salt and black pepper to taste. Simmer, stirring occasionally, while you cook the mushrooms.

2 Melt half the butter in a frying pan and fry the mushrooms for 4–5 minutes. Add the garlic, lemon juice and seasoning to taste. Raise the heat and cook until the mushrooms start to brown. Meanwhile, stir the chopped parsley into the béchamel sauce.

3 Assemble the lasagne. Spread a thin layer of the béchamel sauce in the bottom of a large shallow baking dish. Cover with a layer of lasagne. Add half the mushroom mixture, then a few spoonfuls of béchamel sauce and a sprinkling of Parmesan.

4 Add more lasagne, then half the tomato mixture, followed by béchamel and cheese, as before. Repeat these layers until all the ingredients have been used, ending with béchamel and Parmesan. Dot with the remaining butter. Bake for 30–40 minutes.

Classic Whole Salmon

INGREDIENTS

1 whole salmon
3 bay leaves
1 lemon, sliced
12 black peppercorns
300ml / ½ pint / 1¼ cups water
150ml / ¼ pint / ⅔ cup white wine
2 cucumbers, thinly sliced
mixed fresh herbs, such as bay leaves, parsley, chervil and chives, to garnish
mayonnaise, to serve

SERVES 8–10

1 Preheat the oven to 180°C/350°F/Gas 4. Clean the inside of the salmon and wipe the cavity with kitchen paper. Cut the tail into a neat "V" shape, with  scissors. Calculate the cooking time, allowing 15 minutes for 450g/1lb and 15 minutes over. Place the fish on a large piece of double thickness foil and tuck the bay leaves, lemon slices and peppercorns inside the cavity. Bring up the foil around the sides and pour over the water and wine. Seal the parcel and place in a large roasting tin.

2 Bake the salmon for the allotted time, then remove from the oven, open the parcel and leave to cool. Do not chill the fish overnight or the skin will be impossible to remove.

3 Cut off the head and tail, reserving them for display, if wished. Turn the fish upside down on a board, then peel away the base foil and any excess brown flesh from the pink salmon flesh.

4 Make an incision down the back fillet, drawing the flesh away from the central bone. Carefully transfer one fillet to the serving dish, then remove 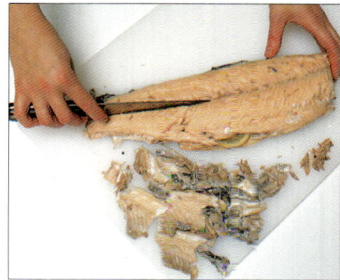 the second fillet and place it beside the first to make the base of the fish. Lift away the backbone.

5 Place the other half of the fish, with the skin intact, on top of the base fish. Peel away the upper skin and any brown bits. Replace the head and tail, if wanted. Decorate with the cucumber slices, overlapping them so that they look like scales. Garnish the salmon with big bunches of fresh herbs and serve with mayonnaise on the side.

Party Desserts

Frozen Raspberry Mousse

Ingredients

350g/12oz/3 cups raspberries, plus extra for serving
45ml/3 tbsp icing sugar
2 egg whites
1.5ml/¼ tsp cream of tartar
115g/4oz/½ cup granulated sugar
25ml/1½ tbsp lemon juice
250ml/8fl oz/1 cup whipping cream
15ml/1 tbsp framboise or Kirsch
mint leaves, to decorate

Serves 8

1 Purée the raspberries in a food processor, then press through a sieve into a bowl, to remove the seeds. Pour about a third of the purée into a small bowl, stir in the icing sugar, cover and chill. Reserve the remaining purée.

2 Combine the egg whites, cream of tartar, sugar and lemon juice in a large heatproof bowl. Place over a saucepan of barely simmering water and beat with a hand-held electric mixer until the mixture is very thick and forms stiff peaks.

3 Remove the bowl from the heat and continue beating the meringue mixture for 2–3 minutes, until it cools slightly. Whip the cream to soft peaks, then fold it into the meringue, with the unsweetened raspberry purée and the liqueur. Spoon into a 1.5 litre/2½ pint/6 cup ring mould. Cover and freeze overnight.

4 Dip the mould briefly in warm water and turn the mousse out on a serving plate. Fill the centre with fresh raspberries and decorate with mint leaves. Serve the mousse with the sweetened raspberry purée.

Cool Green Fruit Salad

Ingredients

3 honeydew melons
4oz / 1 cup green seedless grapes
2 kiwi fruit
1 starfruit
1 green-skinned apple
1 lime
6fl oz / ¾ cup sparkling white grape juice

Serves 6

1 Cut the melons in half and scoop out the seeds. Keeping the shells intact, scoop out the flesh with a melon baller, or scoop it out with a spoon and cut into bite-size cubes. Reserve the melon shells.

2 Remove the stems from the grapes, cutting any large grapes in half. Peel and chop the kiwi fruit. Thinly slice the starfruit. Core and thinly slice the apple and place the slices in a bowl, with the melon, grapes, kiwi fruit and starfruit.

3 Pare the rind from the lime and cut into fine strips. Blanch the strips in boiling water for 30 seconds, then drain and rinse in cold water. Squeeze the juice from the lime and toss into the fruit.

4 Spoon the prepared fruit into the reserved melon shells and chill. Just before serving, spoon grape juice over the fruit and sprinkle it with lime rind.

Host's Tip

If you are serving this recipe on a hot summer's day, serve the filled melon shells nestling on a platter of crushed ice. Not only will this keep the dessert beautifully cool, it will also make it look spectacular.

PARTY DESSERTS

Strawberries with Cointreau

INGREDIENTS

1 orange (unwaxed)
75g/3oz/6 tbsp granulated sugar
150ml/¼ pint/⅔ cup water
90ml/6 tbsp Cointreau or other orange-flavoured liqueur
900g/2lb/6 cups strawberries, hulled
475ml/16fl oz/2 cups whipping cream

SERVES 8

1 Using a vegetable peeler, remove wide strips of rind from the orange, taking care not to include any of the pith. Stack two or three strips together and cut  into very fine strips. Heat the sugar and water in a small saucepan. Bring to the boil, swirling to dissolve the sugar, then add the strips of rind and simmer for 10 minutes. Remove from the heat and leave the rind and syrup to cool completely, then stir in the liqueur.

2 Reserve eight strawberries for decoration. Cut the rest lengthways, into halves or quarters. Put them in a bowl and pour the syrup and orange rind over. Set aside for 2 hours.

3 In a large bowl, whip the cream to soft peaks and sweeten with a little of the syrup from the strawberries. Serve the strawberries in individual glass  dishes, topped with the whipped cream and decorated with the reserved strawberries.

Baked Plum Tart

Ingredients

450g/1lb ripe plums, halved and stoned
30ml/2 tbsp Kirsch or plum brandy
350g/12oz shortcrust or sweet shortcrust pastry, thawed if frozen
30ml/2 tbsp seedless raspberry jam

Filling

2 eggs
50g/2oz/¼ cup caster sugar
175ml/6fl oz/¾ cup whipping cream
grated rind of ½ lemon
1.5ml/¼ tsp natural vanilla essence

Serves 8

1 Preheat the oven to 200°C/400°F/Gas 6. Put the plums in a bowl, stir in the Kirsch or plum brandy and set aside for about 30 minutes.

2 Roll out the pastry on a lightly floured surface and line a 23cm/9in flan tin. Prick the base of the pastry with a fork and line with foil. Add a layer of baking beans and bake blind for about 15 minutes. Remove the foil and beans.

3 Brush the base of the pastry case thinly with jam, then bake for 5 minutes more. Set the pastry case aside and lower the oven temperature to 180°C/350°F/Gas 4.

4 Make the filling. In a bowl, beat the eggs and caster sugar until creamy, then beat in the whipping cream, lemon rind, vanilla essence and any juice from the plums.

5 Arrange the plums, cut-side down, in the pastry case. Pour the custard mixture over. Bake for 30–35 minutes or until the custard has set. Serve warm or at room temperature.

Chocolate Mandarin Trifle

Ingredients

4 trifle sponges
14 amaretti biscuits
60ml/4 tbsp Amaretto di Saronno or sweet sherry
8 mandarin oranges

Custard
200g/7oz plain chocolate, broken into squares
30ml/2 tbsp cornflour or custard powder
30ml/2 tbsp caster sugar
2 egg yolks
200ml/7fl oz/scant 1 cup milk
250g/9oz/generous 1 cup mascarpone cheese

Topping
250g/9oz/generous 1 cup fromage frais
chocolate shapes
mandarin slices

Serves 8

1 Break up the trifle sponges and place them in a large glass serving dish. Crumble the amaretti biscuits over and sprinkle with Amaretto or sherry. Squeeze the juice from 2 mandarins and sprinkle over the biscuit crumbs, then peel and segment the remaining mandarins and arrange them on top.

2 Make the custard. Melt the chocolate in a small heatproof bowl over hot water. In a separate bowl, mix the cornflour or custard powder, sugar and egg yolks to a smooth paste.

3 Heat the milk in a small saucepan until almost boiling, then pour on to the cornflour mixture, stirring constantly. Return to the clean pan and stir over a low heat, until the custard has thickened slightly and is smooth.

4 Stir in the mascarpone until it has melted, then add the melted chocolate, mixing well. Spread evenly over the trifle, cool, then chill in the fridge until the chocolate custard has set. To finish, spread the fromage frais over the custard, then decorate with chocolate shapes and mandarin slices.

Index

Almonds, tapas of cheese, olives & , 18
Avocados: avocado, orange & almond salad, 35
　guacamole with chilli chips, 14

Barbecued mini ribs, 33
Blinis with smoked salmon & dill cream, 28

Carrot, apple & orange coleslaw, 38
Celery sticks with Roquefort, 17
Cheese: celery sticks with Roquefort, 17
　cheese & onion flan, 52
　onion & goat's cheese tartlets, 26
　Parmesan filo triangles, 25
　spinach in filo with three cheeses, 49
　Stilton burgers, 43
　tapas of almonds, olives & cheese, 18
　tiny cheese puffs, 20
Chicken: spicy chicken wings, 29
　tandoori chicken sticks, 32
　tortilla flutes, 48
Chocolate mandarin trifle, 62
Chorizos in red wine, 40
Coleslaw: carrot, apple & orange, 38

Crab dip, hot, 16
Crudités, pepper dips with, 13

Dips, 13–16

Fruit salad, cool green, 58

Garlic: roasted garlic toasts, 24
Garnishes, 11
Guacamole with chilli chips, 14

Lamb: lamb moussaka, 50
　skewered lamb with red onion salsa, 30
Lasagne, baked vegetable, 53

Mediterranean salad with basil, 36
Moussaka, lamb, 50

Olives, tapas of almonds, cheese & , 18
Onion & goat's cheese tartlets, 26

Parmesan filo triangles, 25

Peppers: pepper dips, 13
　roasted pepper salad, 39
Pizza, party, 46
Plum tart, baked, 61
Popcorn, hot & spicy, 21
Pork: barbecued mini ribs, 33
Potatoes: Tex-Mex baked potatoes with chilli, 44

Raspberry mousse, frozen, 57

Salads, 35–9
Salmon, classic whole, 54
Sausage rolls, mini, 23
Smoked salmon, blinis with dill cream & , 28
Spinach in filo with three cheeses, 49
Stilton burgers, 43
Strawberries with Cointreau, 60

Tandoori chicken sticks, 32
Tapas of almonds, olives & cheese, 18
Tarts: baked plum tart, 61
　onion & goat's cheese tartlets, 26
Tex-Mex baked potatoes with chilli, 44
Tortilla flutes, 48
Trifle, chocolate mandarin, 62